I0159197

# LIFE LESSONS

What I learned during my career in law
enforcement… and in life

By

Christina McCalla

**Life Lessons**
What I learned during my career in law
enforcement...and in life

Christina M. McCalla
Copyright © 2012
All Rights Reserved.

## AUTHOR'S NOTE

The scanning, uploading and distribution of this book via the internet or any other means without the permission of the publisher is illegal and punishable by law. Please purchase only authorized editions, and do not participate in or encourage piracy of copyrighted materials. Your support of the author's rights is appreciated.

# Table of Contents

# Introduction

I don't consider my life better or worse than anyone else's. I've endured my fair share of hardships, but I've also celebrated many victories.

I think what sets me apart from most other people is my positive outlook. I try to stay focused on the good things that life has to offer. That can be hard when I'm struggling to understand life's dark side. I've certainly cried many tears trying to remain in faith. But, I'm smart enough to know that some lessons cannot be taught. They have to be learned.

It wasn't until I actually sat to down to make a list of things I want to accomplish in my life that I came up with the idea of writing this book. I self-published my first book focused on helping people achieve weight loss success, but I wanted to take a different approach this time around. I want to motivate, inspire, and hopefully help a broader spectrum of people.

I've decided that it's my life goal to give people hope when they can't see it for themselves. It's my desire to motivate people to use their talents and pursue their dreams; to become the person they've always wanted to be.

I am absolutely determined with every ounce of energy I have in my body to leave this world a better place than it was when I came into it. I intend to do this…one word of encouragement at a time.

I hope that once you've finished this book, you take your dreams and your goals and make them a reality. You may be the next brain surgeon who saves the life of someone I love. Maybe you'll become the scientist or researcher who finds a cure for cancer. Or, perhaps you'll be the one person who ends up in just the right place at just the right time to give one of my family members or friends peace in a time of crisis.

You are the next Change Agent this world needs.

Here are my stories. Some of them I've kept vague to protect those involved. It's more important to me that I respect people's privacy and dignity than it is to "make a story." Regardless, the lessons remain the same. You'll get the point.

# ~ LESSON 1 ~

## People may not remember what you say or do, but they'll always remember how you make them feel

In my "previous life," my life before I was a published writer and author, I was a child support enforcement officer and a Reserve Lieutenant for my local sheriff's department.

What is a Reserve? It's a person who acts side by side with a full time officer with no monetary benefit. I bought my own equipment, donated my time, and put my ass on the line free of charge.

Why? Some days I wondered.

One particular day I was working with the canine unit. I remember that it was Father's Day. That fact stands out vividly in my mind because getting a potential suicide call on any day is horrible. But to get it on what should've been a happy day made it that much worse.

I was extremely familiar with the house that dispatch was sending us to. Growing up, I had practically lived there. Although my friend had moved out years prior, that house held many precious memories for me. I had learned a lot of life lessons there. But this was no time for a trip down memory lane. I had to remain focused on the call.

My mind was racing. It was my first suicide call, so I had many questions. How would I respond if it was in fact successful? Could I handle it or would I be throwing up in the corner like you sometimes hear cops do? Even if I could stomach it physically, would I be able to handle it mentally or would I be fighting nightmares for years to come?

My concerns were silenced quickly as this was no time to think about myself. Our caller was an anxious family member on scene, and they needed our help.

Upon arrival, we found out that the potential suicidal subject had been depressed for quite some time and had come up missing. The family member feared the worst.

We gathered all of the information we could and began our search. Aware that some people want to leave this world but can't do it themselves, we had to be cautious of a suicide-by-cop situation. As an alternative, we were also aware that our presence could startle the distressed person and we would instantly become witness to their final act of attempting to ease their pain. Neither scenario would be good.

Our search was short lived, as we located the subject within minutes. The suicide was successful (I hate to use that term as success seems too positive a statement for an event so pain-filled).

Regardless, the concerned family member needed to be informed that their loved one was gone and their life had been changed forever. While walking from the scene to the house, my heart ached in an unimaginable way for the person inside who was about to hear that their worst fears had come true. How should I say it? How will they react? How would I want to be told? So many questions ran through my head in that three minute walk that seemed like eternity.

In any loss that happens unexpectedly, there are several stages that those left behind go through. There's denial. They don't believe the events that just unfolded before them. "This isn't happening." "I'll just go to bed and when I wake up tomorrow everything will be back to normal."

There is usually anger as they try to rationalize what just happened. Some people yell and scream at the top of their lungs. "WHY?!?" "What the #$%@ just happened?!?"

Obviously, there's depression. There is sadness to the hundredth degree that most of us cannot imagine if we haven't experienced it ourselves. It's an abyss that attempts to suck you in, takes hold, and tries to keep you.

Sometimes there are questions like, "Why didn't I see this coming?" "What could I have done differently to prevent this?" "If I had only_____, this would have never happened."

There are often attempted bargains or pleas such as, "Please God! If you make this right I will never _____ again!" The person left behind offers to give something up or change something about themself just to have life return to some sort of normal, as their "normal" has now forever been altered.

Hopefully in the end there is acceptance. What happened is what it is; nothing more and nothing less. You make peace with it and move on with your life.

I can't remember exactly what was said by either me or the heartbroken family member, but I do remember the intensity of the emotions. For the victim left behind…and everyone else on scene.

Most people fail to realize that cops are people too. Just because we wear a uniform and carry a gun doesn't mean that we're inhuman. We have feelings. We care. We hurt when we see you hurt. We just can't show it…at that time.

After we got everything as settled as we could, we cleared the scene. Other calls were waiting.

I left that house wondering if I had done any good at all. I questioned if I was any consolation to the true victim; the one left behind. Certainly I wasn't able to take away all of the pain, but did I at least help? Even a little? Everyone has their own way of dealing with life's misfortunes and I only hoped that I offered some comfort to a heart that was breaking so deeply.

About a year later, I ran into this person in a local store. I saw them but they hadn't seen me. I almost froze in my tracks. What should I do? Do I escape silently out the door so that the images of that tragic day weren't forced to resurface?

I wanted so badly to go up to the person just to see how they were doing. I needed to know that they were okay and tell them, yet again, that what happened wasn't their fault. There was *absolutely nothing* they could have done. However, I also wanted to respect their privacy. I didn't want to reopen a wound that was surely still in the healing stages.

After some brief internal conflict, I chose to approach the person. I wanted them to know that someone cared. Even though we were in each other's lives only a brief moment in time, I felt like we were connected. That day was forever etched in both of our brains. Certainly, I didn't have to suffer the loss, but I felt like I shared their pain.

I'm glad I made that choice. I was embraced by a hug that reached my soul and held my heart so directly it might as well have been in the palm of their hand. As we both stood in tears, I was assured that life had become livable for them and they were picking up the pieces and working towards a brighter future.

While neither of us could remember exactly what was said or done, they shared that they felt loved, cared for and taken care of when it mattered most. They didn't feel like they were alone.

What did I learn from this tragic event?

I learned that although someone won't necessarily remember what you say or what you do, they will always remember how you make them feel.

So often, we struggle with how we should respond to others when they are dealing with a major crisis, like the loss of a loved one. We don't know what to say, so we don't say anything. Or, we don't know what to do, so we do nothing.

But, reality is, if we are just there to listen, to provide comfort, to let them know they are not alone, that's usually all that matters.

If you truly want to help someone who is struggling and don't know what to do, ask them. "What can I do for you?" Let them guide your response. In the end, they'll know you care. And that is all that matters.

## ~ LESSON 2 ~

## Everything happens for a reason

I know that sometimes it's hard to rationalize this. When someone you love is diagnosed with cancer, how can you say that there is a reason it happened? What good could possibly come from such a dreaded disease?

Well, I don't have an answer for that and I won't even try to defend that position. I will say, though, that I hope that I continue to believe this if I'm ever faced with a diagnosis like that.

All in all, I do think that life is a series of events that overlap and integrate with each other. There are connections that may not be known for days, weeks, months, or years, if ever. This series of events took me a while to figure out but, looking back, it's very clear that everything had to happen the way it did to be where I am right now.

A couple years ago I took a vacation overseas to visit my mom and step-dad. They live in Wales in the United Kingdom. I have been to their house several times so we decided to meet in Spain to mix things up a bit and create some new memories.

In my infinite planning mode, I write a list of all of my assets (bank accounts, etc.) to give to my sister God forbid something happen to me while I am gone. Not that I think that anything *will* happen but I try to be prepared for all circumstances.

Besides, you should always have someone in your life that knows where all your valuable information is (especially if they are beneficiary). If something were to happen to you, why leave loved ones either scrambling to find the information or not even knowing it existed in the first place?

Anyway, I give her the list and explain to her that I hope she doesn't have to do anything with the information. However, in the event that she does, here it is. I am met with quite an unexpected response.

I can't remember exactly what was said (like we just discussed in lesson 1) but, she referenced that she had just spoken to someone in the recent past who told her that they believed she was going to come into a large sum of money soon. It was like being punched in the gut. Was this a sign? Should I cancel my trip?

Pushing my fears aside, I assure her that I am not worth enough money to meet the description of "large sum" and she's going to have to find her money elsewhere. I'm not sure if she's disappointed? I like to think not. Nonetheless, I keep her statement in the back of my mind as I begin my trek overseas. Post 9-11, anything is possible.

There isn't a direct flight to Spain, so I have a layover in Paris. To some, this would be impressive. To me, it is an annoyance. I get antsy in places I am unfamiliar with and layovers make me nervous. I'm definitely not looking forward to having one in a foreign country, especially as a lone traveler.

I did take two years of French in high school, but all I remember how to say is, "It's raining" and "It's snowing." I didn't really foresee that either of these statements is going to help me in my travels.

Luckily I arrive in Paris on time. With almost two hours to find my next gate, there is plenty of time to relax. Soon I will be in Spain, with the travel there behind me. Turns out that it wasn't going to be this easy.

I am informed that the final leg of my flight has been cancelled. The airline personnel have decided to go on strike. They can get me to my destination, but it would require adding another layover and I wouldn't get there until the next day. Ugh!

I am not thrilled, but have no choice other than to accept their conditions. It takes me twenty minutes to learn just enough French to make a call from a payphone. I am finally successful at connecting with my mom, who is already in Spain awaiting my arrival. I give her the flight changes and tell her to pick me up the next day.

One of the privileges of being forced to stay over is being compensated by the airline with a hotel room and dinner. Little do I know that this will begin a sequence of events that change my life forever.

While trying to get to the hotel, I meet another couple from my home state that was in the same position as I. I have never been so happy to see someone wearing a hat with "Detroit" emblazoned on it!

Normally, knowing someone was from Detroit would scare me a little bit as Detroit is known for its high crime and savory character. But, not this day. They are a little familiarity in the midst of a highly chaotic situation.

Four hours and several language barriers later, I finally arrive in my hotel room (which, incidentally is about ten minutes from the airport) and take a nice, hot shower in an attempt to wash my anxieties down the drain with the rushing water.

Feeling better, I go to dinner with my new hometown friends and another gentleman we met at the airport who is also stranded in Paris. He tries to tell me his name several times, but with the heavy accent I can't quite get it right. "That's okay," he says. "Just call me Prince." Prince? Why? "I am a prince from Nigeria."

I, being law enforcement, am of course skeptical of the accuracy of his "profession," so he gladly provides his royalty card. Well, if he has a card, it must be true, right? Yeah, I'm not convinced either. Not that it matters. I could care less who he is or who he thinks he is. He can wear a cape and call himself Superman if he wants. In a few hours, he will be out of my life forever. Or so I thought.

Shortly after dinner, we all decide to make the most of our delay and go see the Eiffel Tower. Feeling safe as there's a group of us, I agree to go. I'm always game for a new adventure.

If you've ever had the pleasure of seeing the Eiffel Tower, then you know it's a magnificent sight. It was nighttime when we went so you could see it from quite a distance. Every so often, the lights flicker causing it to shimmer like an exquisite gold masterpiece. It is beautiful.

Once we purchase our tickets and wait in line, we take the elevator to the top where we can see all of Paris before us. It is truly majestic. That is, until Prince opens his mouth.

Right there, atop the Eiffel Tower, Prince asks me to be his wife. Under any other circumstances, a proposal atop the Eiffel Tower probably would be a dream. In this case, it's creepy.

Needless to say, I say no. Even through all of the considerations and pleas that he makes, from us having gorgeous children, to my hair being braided beautifully for our wedding, and, oh yeah, don't forget to bow when I was before his father.

Sorry buddy, the answer is still no. Non. Nyet. No way!

The next morning can't come quickly enough. After a brief, awkward ride to the airport with my would-be suitor, I say a hasty good bye and am again en route to the comfort and safety of Spain. But, it couldn't be that easy, right?

At my final layover in Oviedo, Spain, I manage to have my suitcase pulled from the plane and searched by local law enforcement. Mine. The only one they remove and search. Why? I am too tired to ask and decide that I'll never know.

Needless to say, I breathe a huge sigh of relief once I arrive to my final destination and am met with the familiar faces of my mom and step-dad. It is nice to see people who aren't crazy or suspect me of illegal activities. (At least I'd like to believe that.)

Fast forward through the vacation (although it had its fair share of numerous twists and turns) to my return to work.

My friends and colleagues have a field day with the story of the proposal from the Prince. It kind of takes on a life of its own. It earns me the nickname "Princess" and several months later I am presented with a crown. I accept it in my best Ms. Universe pose and do a horrible replication of the Queen's wave. Before I know it, my royal picture is on Facebook.

Now, you may think that this is the end of the story, but it actually is just the beginning. As a result of the Facebook photo, and one comment that was made about it, I re-connect with a former classmate; the man who, as it turns out, is the man I have always dreamt of.

Long story, extremely short, we start a friendship which has resulted in him being my true prince. And, I've never been happier…

My lesson learned here is that it took the trip to Spain, the being stuck in Paris and all of the events that followed for everything to fall into place so that I could connect with the person I have chosen to spend the rest of my life with. I could have never seen it at the time, but everything that happened had to happen just the way it did for me to get where I am right now.

I try to remember this as I go through life and face adversities. I may not understand them while I am going through them, but they are part of the master plan to put me exactly where I am meant to be.

Which leads me to the next lesson…

## ~ LESSON 3 ~

## You're exactly where you're meant to be at this moment in time

I believe in fate and destiny (in case you didn't get that from the last lesson). Not that I believe you should just sit back and wait for life to happen because it's predetermined and there's nothing you can do to change it. I think you have to be an active participant in your own life. But, I do believe that our paths are meant to go in a certain general direction, leading us to exactly where we're meant to be.

There was one point in my life that I felt extremely low. I say low not because it was bad, but because it was overwhelming. I was working as many hours as I could in an attempt to pay off debt. I had my full time job, a part time job and was working overtime to boot. I was definitely burning my candle at both ends.

I was having one of those days where everything seems to have a hurdle attached to it. Work is extremely busy and I am doing a bench warrant sweep that night that requires me to be in another county at a certain time. A time I'm not going to meet if things don't slow down.

I keep telling myself that I will be through this time in my life soon. I only have a few more weeks left in the part time position as a corrections officer as the person I am filling in for will soon be returning to work. That will leave me with some time to rejuvenate and recharge my batteries.

I keep reminding myself how far I've come; how much debt I've already taken care of. I am going to get my credit cards paid off, slow down and begin enjoying life a little.

I do my best to hold it all together and I think I am doing a pretty good job. Then, in a blink of an eye, I can't hold it together any more.

I receive a phone call and am told that my part time job is being extended another month. Okay. Time to breathe. I can last another month if I have to.

Follow that by my next call which is, "Oh yeah, and by the way, the home you're renting has been sold. You're gonna have to move."

I'm sure it wasn't said with that much disinterest, but I still feel like I was sucker punched. Not that I didn't know that the house I am living in was for sale. I did. I just didn't expect my career and home life to change so drastically in the same day.

What am I going to do? Where am I going to live? And, how am I going to find time to make all this happen?

I felt completely overcome with life. I *do* believe all of the old sayings like, "That which does not kill us will only make us stronger" and "God doesn't give you more than you can handle." But, come on. Really? Did these theories *have* to be tested with such intensity?

I am not typically an emotional person. That's probably in part to my law enforcement career which tends to leave you a little callus as a survival tool. But I broke down. I can't stop the tears as I feel completely lost about where my life is headed and how I am going to get there.

Right then an angel, and I mean angel, appeared. One of my fellow colleagues shows up right after I get the news about the job extension and needing a new place to live and he offers me a house at a price I can afford.

I almost cannot believe my ears. It was like the dark skies opened up and a ray of sunlight was shining down on me. He offers me the one thing I need at that moment in time…hope.

Even though, looking back, that was one of my darkest moments, I do realize that everything had to happen just the way it did be in just that physical and emotional spot at that moment in time to receive his graciousness. For that, I am certain.

The best part? That house was the best place ever. When I first divorced, I lived in a little one bedroom house. Perfect for me at that point, but very small. Then, I moved to my second house, the one that had just sold, that was a three story. Way too much room, but I couldn't beat the deal.

This house? It was perfect. It was just the right size, in just the right location. It ended up being my favorite place to live.

I try to remember this when I am in the middle of a struggle that I don't understand. There is some reason I am on the path I am on. Someday, if I am lucky, it will all make sense to me. And, maybe I'll never know. I have to accept that as a possible result too.

If I know that a purpose is being served by being in my current situation, I can handle anything. I don't mind having my edges sanded and my life rearranged if I know that in the end I will emerge a stronger, more capable, and better person.

I think it is life's trying times that make us who we are. It's how we handle our difficulties and adversity that determine our character. It is the hard times that refine our compassion, strengthen our resolve and test our endurance.

I don't mind being tested as long as I know that once the test is over, I will have earned a passing grade to advance to the next level...

# ~ LESSON 4 ~

## If you always do what you've always done, you'll always get what you always got

What's the definition of insanity? It's doing the same thing over and over again and expecting different results. Even though it's crazy (no pun intended), we do it all the time.

I first heard this quote from a close friend of mine when we were having one of those deep conversations us girls are known to have from time to time. You know…the ones where you decide how to fix the world. Everyone else's world but your own that is.

Our conversation was centered around our issues with our weight and self-esteem. And, when she said this, "If you always do what you've always done, you'll always get what you always got," it hit me like a ton of bricks.

For as long as I can remember, I have been preoccupied with what I weigh. There are times in my life where I've been at a normal or healthy weight but even then, like so many other people, I still had issues with it.

I've been on and off diets since I was in my very early teens. I can't pinpoint any one event that began my path of counting calories, creating lengthy exercise workout schedules, or becoming scale obsessed, but I know I started awful young.

I can tell you where I was emotionally at any point in time by looking at pictures and seeing what my weight was. If I was at a "normal" weight, I was happy and felt in control. If I was overweight, I was unhappy and trying to hide it. If I was underweight, I was going through a major stressful event.

With weight loss being a billion dollar industry, I've always known that I am not alone. I'd even go as far as to say that there are more of us with weight issues than there are with no weight issue at all. Almost every person I talk to, female and male alike, has a weight goal lower than what their weight is at the current time.

And, I have researched this topic quite feverishly throughout the years. On a quest to ease the battle within myself and hopefully help other people along the way, I obtained my certification in fitness and nutrition and became certified as a personal trainer.

Life got busy and I let my certification expire, but I continued my research and have always kept abreast of the latest and greatest in health and fitness.

If you have a passion for (or obsession with) weight, diet and exercise, then you know that there are tons of varying opinions about how you should live your life. There are suggestions on what to eat, how often to eat, what nutrients you need, what foods help your efforts, which ones hurt and much more. It can all be very confusing as most findings contradict some other finding, so you're left unsure of what is actually good for you and what is "bad."

What I've always found interesting is that even though there is an abundance of information available, as a society our waistlines continue to grow bigger. This leads me to believe that, for most of us, our weight issues have nothing at all to do with food. I believe that it is our mindset, our attitudes and beliefs that matter most when determining what our weight is. That was the inspiration behind the first book I published titled *Rock Solid A.B.B.s (Attitudes, Beliefs and Behaviors) for Weight Loss Success.*

I wanted to share with others what I knew so that they could increase their awareness of why they may have a difficult time reaching their health and fitness goals. I have a desire to pass along all that I have learned and provide people with struggles similar to mine some avenues to follow in their journey to self-acceptance.

I know that my life has been a roller coaster ride of weight, and thus self-esteem, highs and lows. There are times I've wanted off the roller coaster so bad that I fell prey to all of the quick fix advertisements of "Lose 10 Pounds in 10 Days" and "Drop 2 Dress Sizes in 2 Weeks."

I know deep down that these aren't the right way to go about losing weight, but I want it so badly I can't see the forest from the trees. I do know this…if you always do what you've always done, you'll always get what you've always got. Meaning, if you don't change your ways *permanently* then you aren't going to change your weight permanently either.

Quick fixes only give you temporary results. Let me say that again. *If you go for a quick fix, prepare for the results to be short-lived.*

This is a tough pill to swallow. It's like deciding to no longer play the lottery after twenty years of playing it daily because you finally realize that the odds are stacked so far against you that chances are that you'll never win. It's tough to break habits. And, it will break your spirit if you let it.

I say that it's time that we take a stand against people and companies that are trying to sell people on potentially harmful diets and exercise plans. "Diet" is just an offensive four letter word. As offensive as other words that earn a movie an "R" rating.

You may not want to admit it, but to be healthy and free yourself from weight issues, you have to change the way you live. Period. No way around it. Losing weight isn't easy and it isn't fast. It is a process whereby you have to learn how to use food for its only intent: to fuel your body by providing it necessary nutrients and vitamins.

For a short time in my life, I worked for an internationally known weight loss franchise. In training I was presented with the following question: What would you do if you had to deal with emotion without using food? What? Did people actually do that?

This one little sentence has had such a profound impact on me because I am the ultimate emotional eater. Food has always been a tool used to celebrate, comfort, distract and on and on. Basically, food was the solution for everything; good, bad and indifferent.

There was a point in my life when I couldn't remember the last time that I was actually ate out of *physical* hunger. I ate as a result of mental hunger all of the time. There was something my world clearly lacked and when I didn't get it, I ate. I ate to get temporary comfort or distraction from the fact that I didn't feel whole.

Now I am much wiser to this fact. I still have struggles and maybe always will, but my periods of struggle are fewer, shorter in duration, and less intense. Like I always say, "I'm a work in progress."

I will continue to fight the fight to resolve my emotional issues in non-food ways. Let's face it; food doesn't resolve a non-food issue anyway – **ever**. It can't.

Being tired is only rectified with sleep. Thirst is only quenched by drinking. True physical hunger is only satisfied with eating. Emotional upset can only be satisfied by dealing with whatever is causing those emotions to begin with.

If you always do what you've always done, you will always get what you always got. To think anything different *is* truly insane…

# ~ LESSON 5 ~

## Just when you're sure you're right, be prepared to be wrong

My career switch from law enforcement to writing happened in tandem with a move across country. Of course, this meant that I had to leave my duties as a Reserve Officer. Like most officers who are adrenaline junkies, I wanted a "good" last shift.

In police terminology, this means that I wanted lights and sirens and calls that raised my adrenaline to sky high levels. I wanted to go out with a bang (not a firearm bang of course; I'm not that sick).

The last call I went on met these criteria, but in a completely unexpected way.

When I imagined my last call, I thought of being dispatched to an armed robbery in progress or a stolen vehicle chase. Something with some meat to it. What I got was a medical call. And it left me with a lesson I won't forget.

We'd just finished lunch and a neighboring department was being dispatched to an unknown medical call. The victim was passed out and there were children in the home who were scared. Since we happened to be in the neighborhood, my partner advises dispatch that we would respond.

We pull up to a house that had certainly seen better days. It is run down and in desperate need of some TLC. There are kids toys scattered about the yard, lying next to lawn maintenance tools that were laid wherever they were last used.

The front porch is old and worn. Some of the wood is sunken in and in desperate need of repair. Trying to step on only the sturdiest looking boards, we make our way to the front door.

Much like the outside of the residence, the inside is cluttered and unkempt. There are things scattered about. Nothing really has a place. If it does, it certainly isn't in it.

Lying on the floor in the middle of the kitchen is a fairly young man. He's clearly in distress as his body is seizing.

"Probably drugs," I think to myself. I've seen that enough times. Young, healthy people killing themselves by ingesting foreign substances through smoke, needle, or inhalation. It's really sad, but a sign of the times.

Economics are at their lowest and people are hurting. Not everyone deals with stress effectively, so they use aids. The drug of choice for this area is heroin. We have an epidemic of people overdosing, about 1-2 a month.

We approach the patient and try to provide him as much comfort as possible to get him through the seizure. Everything we learned in training says there's nothing you can do to stop the seizure. You just have to prevent them from hurting themselves or someone else in the process.

If you've ever experienced someone having a seizure, you know they have what feels like superhuman strength. Even if they are smaller than you, they can overpower you fairly easily.

In just a matter of minutes, he starts to come out of the seizure and is trying to understand why he is on the floor and why we are invading his space. I am trying to keep him lying down until the paramedics arrive. That is no easy feat.

He keeps trying to scratch me, grabbing at my arms and I swear if he pulls them much harder, my shoulders are going to come out of their socket. I'm no fragile butterfly, but if help doesn't arrive soon, we are going to need two ambulances. One for him and one for me.

I hear the wail of the ambulance in the distance and know that I just have to endure a little longer. The sirens are always a welcome sound on a medical call. The paramedics could provide the patient relief that we just aren't able to supply. We can handle life-saving techniques, but they have the knowledge and tools to give relief from pain and distress.

With the patient receiving necessary medical care, it frees up my partner and I to work on calming the kids and updating the worried wife who had just arrived home from work. Tension is high as his family is trying to understand what happened.

Later that shift, we run into the ambulance personnel who responded to that call. We inquire how the patient is doing. "Fine," they say.

"Drugs?" we ask. Nope. Food poisoning.

"Really?" I think. Wow. I wasn't aware that food poisoning could bring on a seizure. I was way off base on this one.

I learned that day that you can't judge a book by its cover. I have always prided myself in being nonjudgmental. This particular day, I passed judgment. And, I was wrong.

We all have judgments based upon our experiences. We draw on those judgments when presented with similar situations. Sometimes we are right. Sometimes we are wrong.

I try to remember this in other areas of my life. Just because someone is trying to cut me off in traffic doesn't mean that they're an asshole. Maybe they are rushing to the side of a loved one in need. Or, maybe there is some other reason that puts them in a hurry.

If I pass a homeless person on the street, it doesn't mean that they are there by choice. Maybe something horrible happened to them in their life and they weren't blessed with appropriate, healthy coping mechanisms. Maybe they didn't have family and friends there to lend a helping hand.

Keep an open mind when dealing with others. When you "know" you're right, you close your mind to any other possibilities. Most of the time the result of a judgment passed inappropriately is not life or death. But what if it is?

# ~ LESSON 6 ~

## The only thing that stands between you and happiness, is you

Every morning I am faced with a decision. Sometimes I make a good choice. Other times…not so much.

I like to run. Okay, closer to a jog but you get the point. It helps me relieve stress, get my thoughts in order, keep my weight stable, and take in fresh air and sunlight. I find it to be a cure to most anything that ails me.

And, there's a park right around the corner from my apartment that has running paths. The question I have to ask myself every morning is which path to take.

The first path is kind of a dump really and the people there aren't overly friendly. Most of the time they don't even bother to make eye contact as I pass them by. If they do, it's merely to glance my way and then they look away as if absolutely uninterested that I exist.

At the entrance, it is overrun by these ugly little black birds with crazy looking feet. And, they poop all over. Walking through this area is equivalent to walking through a mine field. Sometimes you are successful and make it through unscathed. But, get distracted even a little and your running shoes will hate you.

Make it through the mine field where you have to watch for bombs and enter the zone where you're on the lookout for missiles. Apparently some people can't read the 50 signs scattered around the park that say, "Pick Up Your Dog Waste." Really. Who let's their dog just go to the bathroom on the middle of the sidewalk and leave it? Apparently, a lot of people.

Beyond the bombs and missiles, is the 'bug zone.' Holy swarming gnats! There are millions of these flying atrocities waiting anxiously for you like guests at a surprise party.

You don't dare open your mouth for fear that you'll inhale one of these little menaces into your lungs. I've had them get as far as up my nose. It definitely required some talent trying to kill it while maintaining absolute composure so that no one around me realized that there was a gnat stuck in my snot, fighting for its last breath.

Anyway, make it to the end of the path (which is a circular path that deposits you at the beginning) and you have to go through the mine field yet again before you are able to exit the park.

Now, let me tell you about the other path. It is two miles of paved walkway around a gorgeous lake. The view in the distance is mountains that are absolutely majestic. They are so tranquil. So naturally beautiful.

This path has wildlife but they are exotic birds that are so graceful and elegant floating on the clear still water. Sometimes they play with each other. I swear you can almost see the smiles on their little faces as they frolic around, like children engaged in a game of tag.

And the people there are friendly. Despite the obvious different cultures, they nod and smile as if to say, "Hello, my friend."

I know what you're thinking. Pretty easy choice about which path to walk. But, herein lies the problem. The choice isn't quite what you think.

Truth is, both descriptions are about the same path.

The choice, the decision I have to make, is the way in which I view it.

Some days I walk that park and I love everything about it. I love the sights, the sounds, the smells, and the people. Other days? I don't like anything about it. Nothing about the park itself has changed. It's my attitude that shifted.

Your choice to wake up and make your day good or bad determines what you will 'see' in that day. If you want to see great things and many blessings, that is what you'll see. If you want to see pain and sorrow, then that's what you'll see. It's up to you.

I equate it to driving down the highway and coming upon an accident on the side of the road. If you are so focused on the accident scene (the blood, gore and emergency lights), you see nothing else around you. You miss the beautiful double rainbow off to your left that hovers over a deer standing at a small brook.

There's so much negativity in the world today that it's disheartening. You can't watch anything newsworthy without all of the bad things that people do being splashed across the headlines. There are wars taking place between different cultures, different races, different religions, and different neighborhoods. It's maddening.

But, I do believe that we control how we see the world. Even amidst all the bad that is happening, good things happen every day. Someone saves a life. A young boy rescues his kid sister from a tree she was excited enough to climb up but scared to death to come down. A cop gets a bad guy off the street.

So, my challenge to you is to take each morning and make a conscious choice to make it a great day. Sure, you have struggles. But, put your focus on all that is good and you will see more good in your life.

That's what life is about, isn't it? The good stuff?

## ~ LESSON 7 ~

## Whether you're a victim or a survivor is completely up to you

My grandmother died of cancer when I was about ten years old. I have few memories of her, but the ones I do have are good ones. I remember her as a kind woman, always with a smile on her face. It was her that motivated me to participate in the Susan G. Komen 3-Day breast cancer walk.

Cancer is a dreaded disease. I, probably like you, have had several people close to me fight this disease and win and some have fought the disease and lost. I wanted to do my part to help so that, hopefully in the future, fewer people would have to face this fight at all.

With that, I signed up. I was going to change the world! What I found, instead, is that the world changed me.

The pre-race preparation requires following a training schedule and raising $2,500.00. The walking part would be fairly easy. But, the fundraising? Asking for money makes me uncomfortable. Especially in this economy.

I was amazed and humbled by the number of people who opened their wallet and supported me and the cause. Not only did my family and friends help me raise the minimum, I raised enough to donate to other walkers who were short on their funds! Yay!

With a backpack full of amenities and my walking shoes on, I set out at 4:00 that crisp August morning having no clue what to expect. Sure, I was prepared physically. I had walked daily and went to meetings where they told us what to bring, what not to bring and all of that. But there is no way that I could have prepared for the mental and emotional journey lie before me.

The excitement in the air was electrifying. There was an energy so strong that whatever doubt I had had about finishing sixty miles in three days was gone in an instant. I was going to do this. We, as a whole, were going to do this.

During the course of the walk, I met some truly amazing people. The stories that they shared were incredible. We talked of battles fought against cancer that were won, and battles that were lost. There were tales of heartache and struggle, and tales of strength and perseverance.

One thing was consistent. Everyone walking had hearts of warriors. These were people who weren't willing to say, "I give," or, "I quit." These were fighters!

Sure, there were aches and pains along the way. In fact, I laugh when I think about waking up in the middle of the night, in my tent the size of an airplane bathroom, to the sound of pill bottles rattling all around me, dispensing much needed pain relief for blisters and sore muscles. But, the pain never detracted from the smiles that people had on their faces during the day.

Each day finished carried with it a sense of accomplishment. Day number one was probably the hardest for me physically. The day ended with an ice pack on my knee and a hope that it would feel better during the next two days. It wasn't an option to quit. And I wasn't the only one that felt that way.

On day number three, nearing the sixty mile mark, I came across a woman that was in some obvious pain. She was walking with a limp in both legs. I asked if she was okay and she replied that she knew her feet were bleeding, but she didn't dare take off her shoes. She was sure that if she did, she wouldn't be able to put them back on. She said, "I came this far. I said I'd walk and I'm walking. I am *not* stopping now." The determination she had was so inspiring.

There were many people like that that I met that weekend. Some, like me, had lost loved ones and were walking in their memory. Some were survivors and were walking to show their strength and determination and to walk for others who weren't as physically strong. There were people from all walks of lives, all walking for their own reasons.

At the end, once we had all crossed the finish line, they had this fantastic celebration. We had done it! While I remember being astonished at the amount of money they said we raised (somewhere in the millions), what I remember most is seeing the welcoming faces of my sister and her family there to cheer me on and say how much they supported me and what I had just accomplished.

In life you have two choices. You can be a victim and always walk around feeling sorry for yourself and asking for others to have pity on you. Or, you can be a survivor. You can use your strength, courage, and conviction to help others and to show the world that you will not give up.

I choose to be a survivor. What do you choose?

# ~ LESSON 8 ~

## To fear is normal; to face that fear is what sets you apart

Fear has a way of robbing us of our dreams. How many things have you decided to not do something simply because you were afraid?

I've wanted to be a writer for as far back as I can remember. But I feared failure. So what did I do? I went into law enforcement. Don't get me wrong. I have a passion for law enforcement. And, I have no regrets about my choice. I have learned many great things, had some amazing experiences, and met some fantastic people. It's all good.

But, even though I was enjoying my career, I always felt like something was missing. Writing kept coming back into my mind, but I kept pushing it out. I never said a thing about wanting to be a writer because I was afraid that others would say how stupid I was. It was like saying I wanted to be a famous star. Lots of people do, but reality is that very few make it big.

Besides, I had bills to pay. I had debt to resolve. I didn't have the luxury of doing what I wanted to do. Or so I thought.

Just when I was sure my dream was dead, I was presented with an amazing opportunity. I knew if I didn't take it right then, it would probably be gone forever.

I was born and raised in small town Michigan and, quite honestly, I expected to live there forever. Why not? There's nothing wrong with small town living. I was happy there.

So, when I was faced with the opportunity to move to California, I was pretty taken aback. Me? Leave all I've ever known? You want to talk about fear.

The whole idea of a cross country move would be a major change. I had created a life for myself. Sure, it wasn't rock-star living, but it was comfortable. I had so many people in my world that I treasured. How do I walk away from them?

Then, one day it hit me like a ton of bricks. I was so focused on what I was losing, I failed to realize what I could be gaining. If I made the decision to move, I was opening up great opportunities…like becoming a writer. I still had reservations about how well I would do, but writing for a living became a distinct possibility.

I can't explain the renewed excitement I felt about life. Suddenly, everything began falling into place. It's like by making the decision to pursue my dreams, the flood gates opened. I had always heard that if you do what you love you'll never work a day in your life. I finally realized the truth behind that statement.

During the course of the months leading up to physically leaving Michigan, I wrote whenever I could. If I was awake and not at work I was in front of my computer, pouring my thoughts and ideas on paper.

Through some research (my investigative techniques were put to great use) and helpful tips from others who had walked this path before me, I found a fantastic company that helped me get my book ready for publication. This was really happening to me.

Within months, I had self-published my very first book titled *Rock Solid ABBs (Attitudes, Beliefs and Behaviors) for Weight Loss Success*. I actually did it. I wrote a book! It felt almost surreal.

That gave me the confidence I needed to reaffirm that I was finally, for once in my life, on the right career path. I was taking my dream of becoming a writer and turning it into a reality. Other people did it before me so there was no reason I couldn't do it. Nothing was going to stand in my way ever again of reaching my dreams…not even myself.

Being a realist, I knew when I moved that it was going to take a lot of hard work and effort to reach my goals. Dreams don't just become reality by wishing them so. My hope was to be at least semi-employed within twelve months. I was technically unemployed for two days before scoring my first paying writing job. Things were moving at the speed of light.

Here's why I tell you this story, if I had given in to my fear of failure, my fear of the unknown, you wouldn't be reading this right now.

Fear is nothing but a feeling. Let me say this again…*fear is nothing but a feeling*. It cannot harm you. It cannot take that which you do not give it. It's time to look fear dead in the eye and say, "You will control me no more."

Face your doubts, reservations, and worries. Follow your dreams. I did and I assure you that I am no extraordinary person. I am just a girl who wanted to say, "I did it!" Don't you want to say that too?

# ~ LESSON 9 ~

## When you think you have it bad, look around

There's a story about a woman who had suffered tremendous heartache. Her life was full of loss and disappointment. Her parents had passed; she had no love in her life. She felt all alone. She didn't know how to go on.

In search of a cure for her depression, she went to the town wise man. He listened to her story and told her to find just one person who had life easy, bring them to him and he would cure her.

So she set out on a mission. As she went from home to home, she learned that everyone suffered heartache on some level. In talking with the people she met, they shared stories about what horrible hands they had been dealt. They told her of children stricken with deadly diseases, farms facing foreclosure and lives torn apart. She didn't want them to suffer like her, so she attempted to help them. She offered advice and consoled them. She helped them find the positives in their world.

With each person that she helped she pulled out of her depression a little more. In this she learned the secret to happiness. Help others and you will help yourself.

It can be easy to get caught up in your own situation and forget that the world keeps turning, even if your world has seemingly stopped completely. Everyone endures heartache and pain and your problems can consume you if you let them.

One morning I was running on my treadmill, thinking about how much I didn't want to be exercising. Why did I always have to try so hard to battle my weight? Why couldn't I just be one of those "naturally skinny" people?

After about ten minutes of running, despite my great desire to sit on the couch and watch the morning news with a piping hot cup of coffee, my mind wandered to my friend that had just been diagnosed with cancer. He was in the hospital fighting for his life at that very moment. And there I was, bitching about 'having' to run on the treadmill at 5:00 a.m. No doubt, he would probably have given anything to change places with me. I smothered my inner voice and kept running. Not because I had to, but because I could.

You see the videos of the people who lose limbs or are confined to wheelchairs and yet they are smiling because they feel blessed. They are *my* inspiration. They are the ones that have a reason to sulk and yet they continue their fight with positivity and optimism.

The best cure for a "poor me" mood is to take the time to count your blessings. When I feel myself start to slip into "why me?" mode, I remind myself that my focus is all wrong. My new mantra becomes, "Thank God I'm me!"

Instead of looking at what I feel is wrong with my life, I look at everything that I'm blessed with. Soon, as the depressed woman who consulted with the wise man learned, I start to feel good about my world again as I realize that I really don't have it bad at all.

I encourage you to do the same. For everything bad that happens in your world, you can always find someone that has it worse.

Like my good friend says, "I don't want to wait for something bad to happen for me to appreciate what I have." Very good advice, Amy. Very good advice indeed.

# ~ LESSON 10 ~

## Sometimes trouble *does* come looking for you

I was on my way home from a late night meeting. What should've been a one hour drive was extended due to a reroute because of road construction. (Anyone from Michigan can tell you that the state symbol should be the orange construction barrel.) Anyway, as fate would have it, my detour got me involved in a situation that is just too crazy to be anything but true.

I am a cautious, attentive driver, whether on duty or off. Although I've given way more warnings then tickets, my mom will tell you that if I pulled her over she would get a ticket. I admit it. I still haven't decided if I would ticket her or not. Luckily, I've never had to find out.

This particular night when I am driving home, in my personal vehicle, and I am extra alert because it's not my normal route. I am really concentrating because I don't know the roads. And, it had just quit raining so the roads twists and turns aren't easy to see too far in advance.

I come out of a small town and enter a rural area, and I notice a car in front of me driving erratically. The vehicle is weaving between the yellow line and the white line and the speeds are going from nearly crawling to excessively fast. Assuming the driver is tired, intoxicated, or having a medical issue, I got my cell phone out to call it in.

When we're both stopped at a stop sign, I'm able to get a good vehicle description (I'm not the best at vehicle makes and models) and a plate registration. I make the 911 call. I am in my own county and know the dispatcher so I am giving her the information in the same manner as if I was on duty.

I figure it will be a normal call which will end in me giving her our direction of travel. She will dispatch a BOL (be on the lookout) and, hopefully, there's a patrol car in the area that can intercept this vehicle and check out the driver. If not, I feared that they would hurt themselves or someone else. If there is one thing I've learned in all of my police training, there is no such thing as "normal," so I should've known better.

Two minutes later, we're at the next four way stop and I'm right behind the vehicle again. I am still on the phone with dispatch when the car in question doesn't move. It isn't turning right or left and it isn't going straight. It just sits.

I watch it for a minute to see what's going on. Is the driver having a medical issue? Is there more than one person in the vehicle and they're having an argument?

After what seems like forever, the driver, who I can see is female, starts to flag me around her. "What's going on?" I think to myself. I pull cautiously to her left and roll my passenger side window down. The woman, who reeks so heavily of alcohol I can smell it in my vehicle, states she is lost and wants me to give her directions. I tell her it's best if we move our vehicles out of the middle of the intersection first. Luckily, she agrees and I follow her to the side of the road just beyond the intersection.

With dispatch still on the phone, I tell them exactly where we are and hope I can keep the driver there long enough to get an officer on scene. Anyone who's ever been around someone who is drunk knows that they can be pretty easy to entertain, but they can also be pretty unpredictable. This one turned out to be a bit of both.

I exit my vehicle and engage in conversation with the driver of the other car who is clearly having a hard time standing. She is trying to get her bearings on where she is and wants me to help her get "un-lost."

She tells me her starting point and also informs me where she is trying to end up. It's a drive that should've taken her ten minutes. Yet, here she is, about an hour and a half from her initial location and just as far from her destination. How this woman got this far without killing herself or someone else is amazing.

The whole time we're standing on the side of the road, the woman is just babbling away. And she laughed and laughed. She was quite amused with herself. And, I must admit, I was quite amused with her also. At least I had a happy drunk, which was definitely more pleasant than the alternative.

As she was jabbering, she must've told me twenty times how glad she was that I wasn't a cop. She didn't need that kind of hassle. All I could do was put my best acting face on and tell her that she certainly was lucky. She just had no clue that my idea of luck and her idea of luck fell on different ends of the spectrum. And, within minutes, her luck was about to run out.

When the patrol car pulls up, she suddenly became quiet for the first time since we stopped. She knew she was in trouble. But that wasn't going to stop her from trying to talk her way out of it.

The officers approach, we smile at each other and she starts telling them her story of how she was just driving home and got turned around. The officers asked her the same questions I had just asked and drew the same conclusion. It was amazing that this woman made it anywhere safely. She has no idea where she is and has no business being out on the road in this condition.

"Have you been drinking?" they asked. "Nooooo," she slurred. "I'm just lost." Well, everyone knew that was untrue, her too I would suspect. So, after failing her sobriety tests, she was told that she was under arrest for driving while intoxicated and was going to spend the night in jail. Her only request? To let her put on underwear as she wasn't wearing any. Lucky for her there was a pair right on her passenger seat.

As the officers were placing her in the back seat of the patrol car, she thanked me for trying to help her. I told her it was certainly no problem and I wished her as good a night as she could have.

I never wish anyone bad times and she was no exception. However, she definitely shouldn't have been driving that night and I would've never forgiven myself if she hurt herself or anyone else. She made a bad decision and I did what I had to do as a result.

My colleague later told me that they informed her on her ride to jail that I was an off duty cop. Turns out she didn't like me so much after all. She apparently had a few names to call me. I never got called to court on that case so she must've taken her lumps and moved along. Okay by me.

It's funny how things happen when you're in the right spot at the right time. Had there not been a detour, I would have never been in that area that night and who's to say what might have happened had she continued to drive. Or, she could have pulled over someone who had not so good intentions. I'm not saying it to say that I am some sort of saint or martyr. I am just saying that I was fortunate to be in the position where she was able to get a second chance. I hope that she will make better decisions next time she decides to drink and stay out from behind the wheel of a car.

No matter how much you try to avoid trouble, sometimes it comes looking for you and you have no choice but to say, "Yes. I am here. What can I do for you?" And, as long as you learn from it, then nothing is lost.

# ~ LESSON 11 ~

## There's no such thing as try; either you do or you do not

I've held many jobs in my life. Throughout junior high and high school, I waitressed, cooked and did dishes at a local restaurant that my mom also worked at. I also helped my dad at his terrarium business. Terrariums are little glass and mirror containers that you plant different plants in and use colored sands and bark pieces to make little nature scenes.

At age eighteen, I graduated to bartending. I could write a whole book about my experiences doing that, but it wouldn't be suitable for all ages. Suffice it to say that I learned a lot, but most of what I learned was either useless or appalling. It wasn't all bad though. I did learn an awful lot about football and the best way to cook ribs.

After I graduated from high school and college, I've always held part time jobs in addition to my full time job. On top of being a child support officer and Reserve Officer, I spent time working for an attorney doing secretarial duties, cleaned out houses after evictions, worked for a weight loss franchise, conducted NRA home defense classes and krav maga self-defense classes and I know there's a couple more jobs I'm forgetting. If something interested me and I had time, I did it.

In honesty, if I had my way, I would've held six professions. I'd be a police officer, lawyer, psychologist, writer, professional dancer, and singer. I guess I've satisfied the police officer and writer avenues. I used lawyer and psychology skills in dealing with clients. I'm still trying to figure out the dancing and singing part. Stay tuned on that.

Anyway, one of the consistent themes I see, no matter what job function I am doing, is that people have excuses for everything. There is a major lack of responsibility for personal choices and situations.

"Why don't I pay my child support? I can't find work." "I was speeding? Really? I hadn't noticed." I am so sick of hearing excuses. People have reasoning for everything they do. While, granted, some are valid, most of them are not. What happened to taking responsibility for our choices? It's time to say, "Yes. I did it. I was wrong."

I talk with people all the time who struggle with issues that prevent them from reaching their goals.

And how they answer my questions tells me how committed they are in making changes. For instance, if I suggest a solution and their response is, "I will try," I know that chances of them reaching their goal are slim to none. Those three words, "I will try," are so self-defeating. Either you do or you do not. You cannot try.

I watched a video of Tony Robbins, famous motivational speaker, teaching this very concept to an audience of people. He apparently feels the same way about the word "try" as I do. He had a woman who clearly lacked any responsibility for her current situation. She used the excuse that she tried to make it better but it didn't work.

To drive home his point, he told her to *try* to move her chair. When she picked it up to move it, he stopped her. He hadn't told her to move it. He told her to *try* to move it. She sat the chair down and he gave her the same directive again. Try to move it. She started to move it and again he stopped her. Once more, he explained that he did not want her to move the chair. He just wanted her to *try* to move it.

She was so caught up in her current thought process that she was missing his lesson. This went on several minutes with her frustration increasing.

Finally, he stopped her and explained the lesson. You cannot try. Either you do or you do not.

Put it to the test yourself. Say, "I will *try* to (insert goal here)." Now, say, "I *will* (insert goal here)." Do you see the difference?

While we're on the subject of wording, the same is true for using the word "if." For instance, it's pretty common to hear, "*If* I lose ten pounds I will feel better." Now, replace that sentence with, "*When* I lose ten pounds I will feel better." See how one is a dream without action and one is a solid commitment?

How you talk to yourself matters. If I give myself an out, I'll take it. But if I start from a position of strength, by using phrases like "*When* I…" or "I *will*…" half of the battle is already won. I've told myself that I will succeed so my mind sees no other option.

Now I know you're saying, "Well what if I attempt to succeed and don't?" If you make a plan, try it and it doesn't work, modify your attempt, switch your tactics, and try again. Just because you don't succeed the first time, using a certain route doesn't mean that you shouldn't pursue your end goal. You just have to take a different road to get there.

It's like the invention of WD-40. Do you know where it got its name? It's because the inventor didn't get it right until his 40th attempt. So you don't get what you want the first time. That's okay. Just don't let it stop you.

And, if you catch yourself saying that you'll *try* to do something, stop yourself and rephrase it. Commit to it. Make it happen.

# ~ LESSON 12 ~

## Blood isn't always thicker than water; especially when your sister attacks you

I love my sister. I really do. So when she viciously attacked me, I was shocked!

Okay, maybe that's not exactly how it went, but I hope she was taken aback when she read it. She deserves every bit of smack I can give her and let me explain why.

As I mentioned in a previous lesson, I was trained in the krav maga form of self-defense. Krav maga is an Israeli form of defense where the moves are executed with speed and force. It's superior to any form of self-defense I've ever learned.

Traditional self-defense involves complicated moves that you'll never remember unless you practice them religiously, which most people don't. Krav maga focuses on moves that are instinctive, making them easier to remember and execute.

Also, most self-defense classes teach you to defend yourself from the attack and then run. It's a good principal because you don't want to wait around for more problems, but the suspect is able to keep the upper hand and that's not good.

Krav maga teaches you to defend yourself and to counter-attack with speed and force. This leaves your opponent stunned and transfers the control of the situation from them to you. Talk about empowering!

After receiving excellent instruction from Rick Seid, founder of the Fighting Chance programs, those of us who were certified as trainers decided it was time to hold our own classes. We wanted a class of people to attend a session and give us feedback so that we were sure we could effectively teach what we had learned. And, who's more honest than family and friends, right?

So, I invite my sister, cousins, and a few friends to a free session of self-defense in exchange for their honest opinion and helpful suggestions. Great in theory, but I'm sure you can see what's wrong with this thought. Wish I had seen it...

Let me set the scene for you. We're in one of the trainer's basement and all of us instructors, three in total, are pumped on adrenaline and excited to share our knowledge after having practiced for months.

We each have two people that we are to teach. I have my sister, who is eleven months older than me, and my cousin, who is about ten years younger.

Now, I'm not very tall, just under 5'3, but I am fairly strong and pretty solid. I have been trained in defensive maneuvers for years, both in classes and in my law enforcement training. I am not saying this to say I'm Barney-Badass, just that I have a level of skill I am comfortable with and confident in.

Then there's my sister and cousin. Both ladies are small framed with no defensive background whatsoever. They're kind, loving, generous people who would give you the shirt off your back if you needed it. Hell, my sister donated her kidney for crying out loud. So, to me, they were the perfect students. But, what I soon learned was that beneath that giving exterior, they are laced with enough attitude to take on an army of attackers…and win.

When training begins, I inform my sister that I want her to practice the moves without actually making contact with me. I believe I even asked if she understood what I meant, to which I got a laugh as a reply. Red flag number one.

After we got through the basics, one of the first moves I teach her is a response to a frontal attack. The "victim," my sister, is to take her elbow and move it laterally toward my head. If it were a true attack situation, this move would stun the attacker, allowing you to continue your counter-attack and then get safely away.

I get into position and engage my attack. My sister responds as instructed, other than she makes contact. With my cheek bone. It kind of stings, my eyes water, and she does the only thing she could do...laugh.

I shake my head, came to my senses a little bit, and assure her that she has that move down pat. I remind her again that the goal is to practice the move *without actually making contact*. Her response? Laughter. Red flag number two.

Next move is an attack from behind. Her response is to swing her elbow back toward my head. I am a little leery but, certainly with her nursing background she would certainly understand the importance behind keeping head shots to a minimum.

As we are just starting out, there is no protective head gear for me. Just a promise that she would follow my directions. Uh huh.

I attack and back comes her elbow. Contact number two. I feel and hear my jaw bone crack. This time, my eyes water much harder and I feel an even greater twinge of pain. God bless my sister for being an over-achiever.

She offers an apology, which I can barely understand because she is bent over laughing so hard. While delivering her heart felt sympathies for my pain, I am bent over too. But, for me, it is only in an attempt to clear my head from the ringing that is now clouding my ability to hear at all.

I'd like to believe that she is somewhat sincere in her apology. I do think she kind of feels bad that I can't see through the water that is uncontrollably coming out of my eye sockets. So, I again assure her that she is an A+ student and I am glad that she is picking up self-defense so easily.

Of course, by now she has somewhat of an audience when she is practicing her moves. I don't know if everyone wants to see if she will actually make contact with me again or if they want to see my response. Either way, I can't get her to quit snickering long enough to figure it out. Red flag number three.

Continuing with our attacks from behind, I come at her and place her in a bear hug. Now, at this point, I am not hesitating playing the attacker at all. I am using all of my strength because her frail image is definitely gone from my mind. She responds just as instructed. Kind of. She gets her arm free and brings her elbow back in an attempt to go for my nose.

In a real life self-defense situation, the nose makes a great target because it is a sensitive area that cannot be strengthened by an attacker. Apparently, it makes a great target in a self-defense scenario too. She *does* make contact (surprise), causing such a loud noise when my nose cracks that the whole room stops. At least I think it did. I can't see a thing, but it got very quiet. That was the grand-daddy of all hits. And, the conclusion of our training.

Six weeks later, I'm in the doctor's office because I can't breathe out one side of my nose and it's still painful to the touch. Tests revealed that she had in fact broken my nose.

We reminisce at many family gatherings about that day. And, of course, my version and her version differ slightly. However, one fact remains the same. I still can only breathe out one side of my nose.

Thank you, Caryn. And you can quit snickering any time.

# ~ LESSON 13 ~

## Words paint pictures, but sometimes the pictures are distorted

I love working warrant sweeps. To take someone who is eluding the system and track them down, bringing the victim a little justice? That's my passion. It's up to the court what they do with them after that. It's just my job to get them in.

I spend countless hours beforehand tracking people down, searching for them or someone who might know where they are that would be willing to give them up. Information I obtain is assembled with pictures of the suspect and disseminated to those of us working the actual warrant sweep. We dissect the county into areas and each team takes a section.

To make it a little more interesting, we make a game out of it to see which team can apprehend the most suspects. We all have our own ideas on how to beat the other teams. Some are in stealth mode, taking blacked out vehicles and sneaking up on the subject. Some try the direct approach. They take a fully marked patrol vehicle and walk right up to the front door. Me? I'm lucky. I'm female.

Most people will open their door for a female. And, I'm not in uniform so I'm not a threat. When my partner is another female officer, we rock. We win every sweep we work together, earning us the title of Thelma and Louise. Honestly, I can't remember who is who but I definitely have her back and without a doubt she has mine too.

This one particular sweep I'm partnered up with a couple of male officers who are real go-getters. There's no stopping them once they get on a mission. This gave us a definite advantage over the other teams.

As we're working our way down our list of targeted suspects, we go to a residence to see if our information that the suspect resided there was any good or not. We pull into the driveway and a couple of guys are by a bonfire in the back yard.

We make contact with them and start asking questions. We are looking for a man by the name of Rodney. Nope. Neither of them is Rodney. They are James and John, and they're just trying to relax with some beers by a nice warm fire. Unfortunately, we don't have a picture of this suspect, so we can't say for sure whether one of these guys is him.

One of my partners stays by the bonfire, and my other partner and I go to the house, which turns out to be two separate apartments. Occupants of the lower apartment confirm that one of the guys by the fire is in fact Rodney.

Just as I'm starting to pass that information on to my partner, I see a figure running toward the back fence. It's Rodney, and my partner is right on his heels. Needless to say, Rodney's beer drinking hindered his getaway as he wasn't in any condition to be a stellar athlete that day. In no time, he is being escorted to our car, cuffed, and defeated. When asked why he ran, he replies he was just going out back to pee. Must've had to go real bad.

The next day I meet with Rodney at the courthouse. I am taking him before the court so that the judge can decide poor Rodney's fate. Usually when I go out on sweeps my hair is in a ponytail and I am wearing blue jeans and a t-shirt. In court, obviously, it's different attire. Different enough that people don't always put it together that I was the one that arrested them the night prior.

I never say anything about being the arresting officer because, quite frankly, it's irrelevant. Besides, it's kind of funny when some people give me their version of the arrest. People who ran from me try to convince me that they didn't run and people who resisted arrest try to tell me that they didn't. Little do they realize that I was there, saw it all with my own two eyes, and was part of the festivities.

The judge was ready to see all of the arrestees, so we pile them all in the security elevator and head for the second floor. Between them, me and another court officer, we can't pack one more person in there if we try.

Rodney looks at me, all serious and says, "You look different with clothes on." Ouch. I turn every shade of red imaginable. Of course, I know what he means, but by the jaws that dropped on everyone else, it's pretty clear where their minds went. The picture Rodney painted with his words was pretty vivid!

So often, what is said and what is heard are two very different things. Just as artists find with their art, interpretation is everything. The same is true in life in general.

Someone says something and we get all bent out of shape because we interpret what they said incorrectly. Then, we get so caught up in being "right" that we fail to see that we're both right. Like the famous quote from *Cool Hand Luke*, "What we've got here is (a) failure to communicate!"

The lesson? If someone who is important to you says something hurtful or offensive, take the time to slow down and look at why they said it. You may see that what they said isn't necessarily what they meant.

Most of the time when someone shares their thoughts or opinions with us it is because they care and/or they are trying to help. Or, maybe they're just stating what they see but they don't choose the best words to say it. Like that day in the elevator...

# ~ LESSON 14 ~

## Never underestimate your opponent

Sometimes you can assess someone else's skill. When you can't, that's when it goes all wrong.

Working in law enforcement it's easy to get a big head sometimes. You have access to great training and you feel confident that you can deal with most anything that comes your way. Let's face it, if you don't feel confident, you shouldn't be out on the street. Self-doubt will get you killed.

I've been known to learn things the hard way. I admit that. But, when someone *helps you* learn the hard way, well, it goes from bad to worse quicker than a Tesla Roadster.

We are at training learning how to defend ourselves from knife attacks. An opponent with a knife is just as dangerous as someone with a gun, especially if they are within 21 feet of you. It's a proven fact that they can kill you with their knife before you can even draw and shoot your gun. Even if you expect the attack.

This was the lesson we wanted to teach the other reserve officers. So, my mentor trainer, a Sergeant whom I have nothing but the utmost respect for, discreetly places the knife in my hand and tells me to run at one of the trainees as quick as I can. We are going to hit this lesson home.

I smirk. That sounds like fun to me. I can 'kill' him before he can even respond. I always like role-playing in scenarios, especially if the end resulted in my winning.

I run through it in my mind first. I imagine that I take off at a dead run toward my target. He sees me coming and freezes for a second, just long enough for my knife to mock-penetrate his chest.

I walk away like a proud rooster strutting while he is left, heart pounding hard, being mocked by the other officers for letting a "girl" take him out. Yes, this was going to be a good one. Or so I thought.

It starts out just like I had pictured. I take off toward my "victim" at a dead run. My trainer watches as he is the only one who knows what I am doing. I can all but see the pride in his face as I will certainly earn a spot among the top reserves with this move.

I see my opponent's eyes when he registers what is happening. In that brief millisecond I am reading his thoughts. "What is she doing? She's running straight at me. She has a knife!" I still have a smirk on my face, that is, until he wipes it right off. Or, should I say knocks it off.

Here comes the important part. What my trainer failed to tell me is that my 'opponent' is former military. Retired Captain, to be specific. So, all of the wonderful training I had received up until that point didn't mean squat compared to the amount of defense training he had under his belt.

He stops the attack alright. His elbow to my face (do you see a pattern here?). Yep, didn't quite end the way I envisioned.

Not only did I learn to never run at anyone with a knife in my hand before I knew their background, I learned to never underestimate your opponent. I had trained with this guy for years, yet I was completely unaware of his military background. People rarely wear their past on their sleeves.

I try to remember this in my everyday dealings with people. Whether I've known them for a day, a month or ten years, it's impossible to know their entire background. A background that causes them to respond to situations based on their experiences.

The same is true for complete strangers. I don't know what they've been through. I don't know the struggles they have survived or are dealing with at this moment at time.

Why is this important? Because people respond based upon that which they know. We may both encounter the same issue and respond in a completely different manner because we interpret it differently due to our backgrounds and our experiences being what they were.

This also means that our response say more about us and what we've been through than it does about anyone else. So, you can't take what anyone says or does to you personally. Their actions tell you about them, not about you.

Remember this when you deal with people. We are all students of life. And, no matter how well you know someone, you may never really know everything about them. Don't underestimate them or you may find yourself in a predicament that you never saw coming.

# ~ LESSON 15 ~

## Develop, and keep, your sense of humor

There must be a gazillion jokes out there about cops and donuts. We've all heard them. What is truly amazing is the amount of people that think it is funny to tell donut jokes to cops, like we've never heard them before. Some people try to get a rise out of us just to see what we'll do. Others truly mean to insult us. But, most often, people just think they're being funny. Ha. Ha.

It's always been a little ironic for me because my aunt owns a bakery – the North Branch Bakery in North Branch, Michigan. There is *no better place* to go to get your sugar fix. So, if you're ever in town, it is definitely worth a stop! Her cinnamon rolls are the size of hub caps and the sugar cookies melt in your mouth. Yum!

The busiest day in the year for her is Paczki Day. It's a polish holiday, also known as Fat Tuesday, the day before lent. Due to the huge number of Paczki orders the bakery receives for Fat Tuesday, they have to start making them on Sunday evening.

It's amazing to see how this little, small town bakery the size of a postage stamp is able to produce and distribute over 12,000 of the jelly or custard filled delights in a thirty-six hour time frame!

Between family and friends, there are people constantly coming in to help. They throw on an apron on and jump right in. Whether it's preparing the dough (which is affectionately known as "Bertha" due to the resemblance to big Bertha's belly) before it's fried, or rolling the pastry in massive amounts of powdered sugar at the end, everyone serves a purpose.

Not only do I help, but many other officers who have become close family friends lend a hand too. Plus, some of the guys on duty stop in to check out the festivities. It's pretty safe to say that the bakery is the safest place in the county to be the last few days before Lent begins.

And, due to the heavy police presence, every year, without fail, I hear the same jokes over and over again. Like, "What does DARE mean? DARE to keep cops off donuts." Or, "What are you doing pulling me over? I thought the donut shop was running a sale this morning?"

I've learned that a sense of humor goes a long way. Some officers take great offense at cop and donut jokes. I don't...anymore. I used to despise them. I would cringe and stand up for my profession. "Donut shops serve coffee 24 hours a day. That's why police officers go there," I'd respond defensively.

Then I realized that it wasn't worth my time to be upset about it. I like a good lawyer and doctor joke just as much as the next guy. And, I like when a lawyer and doctor can laugh at them. It doesn't mean that I respect them any less.

Heck, some cops with senses of humor took the cop and donut connection one step further and opened their own bakery in Clare, Michigan called Cops & Doughnuts. Yep, I've been there. I got a t-shirt. Definitely a good stopping point if you're ever in the area.

Of course, I'm blonde and I get to hear those jokes too. And, yes. I even understand them. I like to laugh. If you can't keep a sense of humor about life, then how much fun is it to live?

If you're going to survive the rotten and gruesome things that you see when you're out on the streets, you damn well better learn to keep your sense of humor. If you don't, the darkness and despair will chew you up and spit you out like a piece of well-done meat.

Laughter is a good coping mechanism. It lightens life when it seems a bit too tough. It relieves stress. It improves bonds between people and creates fun memories.

So make it a goal to laugh as often as possible. Find the funny in life's situations. Oh yeah, I haven't heard any good jokes about writers yet, so if you have one please send it my way.

## ~ LESSON 16 ~

## Even if you don't know exactly what to do, at least do something

We've all seen it. Something major or tragic happens and they are surrounded by a crowd of people. People who do nothing but watch. And, occasionally, one or two people step in. Most often they say, "I had no idea what I was going to do but I had to do something." This is dedicated to them, their bravery, and their commitment to taking action.

I was fortunate enough to have the opportunity to go overseas and work road patrol with some of their police agencies. I've worked with City of London and Metropolitan Police in London, England and I've worked with Bermuda Reserve Police. But, nothing holds a match to my patrol with South Wales Police, also in the United Kingdom.

I was on duty with a Special Constable, which is similar to our reserve officers. They also donate their time, but their duties and responsibilities are much different than mine. In order to work, I have to be with a full time partner. Not in South Wales. They are out on the street alone. They act as a full time officer, but without the pay. Now there's commitment.

During our patrol, my newly assigned partner shows me some local trouble spots and tells me how some of the area residents treat law enforcement. As we drive down the street, people yell things at us. Although I have no clue what they are saying due to the heavy accent and being unfamiliar with their slang, the tone pretty much said it all. We are not wanted.

That was an odd feeling for me. Although I know not every person in America respects law enforcement, overall, we have a good relationship with the people we are there to help protect. It opened my eyes that the same is not true all over the world.

There was one area we drove through that was extremely anti-police. Apparently, the locals would often throw bricks at passing patrol cars. I was praying that we didn't get a call in that area at about the same time that our first complaint came across the radio,

Now, at this point in my career, I had been in law enforcement in the states for approximately five years. So, while I wasn't a seasoned veteran, I certainly wasn't a newbie either. I was somewhere in between.

I had the skills necessary to do my job and I felt pretty comfortable in my abilities. However, I soon realized that it's a whole different ball game to be thrown into an area you didn't know, with people you weren't familiar with, lacking the tools you normally use. Talk about a fish out of water.

In several foreign countries, police do not carry firearms like they do in the United States. Wales is one of those countries. So, there I was. No gun. No pepper spray. No baton. Just me, my handcuffs, and my flashlight.

So, when the call came to us, I have to admit that I was a little concerned. Here we are in a rotten area in the middle of God knows where with minimal defensive tools.

To make matters worse, I didn't know the codes they were using on the radio. Not like it would've mattered much if I did because I was having a difficult time understanding their accent anyway. They might as well have been speaking an entirely different language because that's how it sounded to me.

My partner informs me that the radio traffic is for us to respond to a call that every police officer dreads to hear – Officer Needs Assistance. You have a friend, partner, brother or sister in trouble and you need to get there quick.

It's like when a parent hears their child scream. Your heart pounds, your stomach drops and all you can think of is whether or not they are okay. You rush to their side, ready to take on whatever is threatening their safety.

We are flying down unfamiliar streets and I am utterly lost. I can't tell if we're going north, south, east, or west. All I know is that we need to get where we are going as fast as we possibly can.

One of the key pieces of information that my partner relays to me is that the officer in need of assistance is undercover. What? How on earth am I supposed to know who was who between cop and perp? It would have been easy enough at home because I knew all of the officers, but not here. What had I gotten myself into?

I was thinking about the different policing styles, what was proper protocol for them versus what would have been proper for us in the states, as we were pulling on scene. What am I going to do? What *can* I do? I don't have my normal arsenal of weaponry to back me up so I needed to think outside the box and prepare myself.

As soon as our car stopped, my partner takes off in a dead run. Where he was going, I had no clue, but I know I have to keep up. I had learned toward the beginning of our shift that he is an avid runner. Please legs, don't fail me now…

I also know that if we're separated and I get lost, I'm stuck. I have no radio and no idea where I am. So, even if I had a radio I would have a difficult time directing someone to me. I would be toast.

Luckily, it all worked out. No one got hurt and I made it home at the end of the shift. Thank you, God!

This taught me a very valuable lesson. Even if you don't know what to do, you better be ready to do something. Maybe this is an extreme scenario being potentially life or death, but the same holds true any time we aren't in our comfort zone. A lot of people shy away from stepping in or taking action because they are unclear of what to do. But, I tell you this much, if I was getting my butt kicked on the side of the road, I would want you to at least try to help. Don't just stand there and watch, please.

Today is a different day and age. People are sue-happy and that creates a huge fear of response. I understand that and I can't say there aren't times I don't feel the same way. But, to do nothing when someone else is in need is negligent in my books. Remember that the person in need of help is someone's mother, father, brother, sister, daughter or son. How would you want someone else to respond if it was your family member in need?

# ~ LESSON 17 ~

## Always smile because you never know who's watching

It was one of those days. One of those mornings really, since it wasn't even 8:00 AM yet. Everything that could go wrong did.

When working for the court, I would usually set my alarm for around five. This way I had time to get in some cardio exercise, check my email, and not rush around before going to work. Some days the extra sleep would have been nice but, overall, I prefer being productive at home before having to be productive at work.

This particular morning, my preference didn't matter. I set my alarm the night before alright. I even set it for the right time. Didn't matter though since I failed to actually turn it on.

I woke up to sunshine beaming in my window, which was never a good sign in my book. My heart racing, I looked at the clock. Good. It's only 6:30. Sure, I'll have to shorten my normal morning routine but I wasn't going to be late for work. Whew! I always have dreams about being late for work or showing up missing an article of clothing. Is that normal? Never mind. Forget I asked. Neither scenario ever happened so I guess it doesn't really matter.

I jumped in the shower and got ready in record time. My lunch was packed, my paperwork was ready to go, and I even had about five minutes to spare. Just enough time to check my email.

I turn my computer on only to have it decide that it was an appropriate to do a virus scan. Ugh! No email today. I guess I wasn't meant to know what was in my inbox.

I jump in my car only to remember that I need gas. Right. I forgot about that. No worries. I'll grab it real quick and be right on time for work. I have the philosophy that if you're not early, you're late, but I will take just being on-time today because that's the best I was going to get.

I stop at the gas station and use the slowest pump known to man only to try to pay by using a credit card machine that seems to not be working. Wow. I wasn't going to get any breaks no matter how hard I tried.

I make it to work with not even thirty seconds to spare. I walk in the door hurried and scattered. My mission is to get to my desk and get on with my day. It's time to put this rotten morning behind me.

As I'm walking at a brisk pace through the front doors of the building toward my office, I pass a man around my grandfather's age in the corridor. I glance at him, smile, and say hello.

I don't really think much of it as its pretty normal for me to say hi when I pass someone in the hall. Besides, my mind is more on my morning events and hoping that my day was going to turn around.

I am probably two steps past the man when he says something that stopped me dead in my tracks. He says, "You have a really nice smile."

I stopped dead in my tracks, turned and looked at him with an even greater smile that I had when I initially said hello. That was one of the nicest things I had heard in quite some time.

The expression and smile on his face told me he was being absolutely genuine in his compliment. He thought it and wanted to say it. In that instant, everything about my morning that was wrong vanished.

I thanked him for the kind words and we both turned and went our separate ways. That man, with those six words, took all that was bad in my world that morning and made it good. I have thought about that incident so many times over the years. I would give anything to find that man again, talk to him, and tell him what a difference he made. Not only did he brighten my morning, but he reminded me of a valuable lesson. Always smile because you never know who is watching.

Sometimes we get caught up in our own little world and forget that what we do has an impact on those around us. And, we forget that a small act of kindness goes a long way.

I try to pass that kindness along whenever I can. If I see someone and a genuine compliment comes to mind, like if they are wearing a top that accents their eyes, or if they have on a piece of jewelry that is beautiful, I say it. If I see someone do an act of kindness for someone else, I acknowledge it. If they go out of their way to help someone else, I thank them. Even if the person on the receiving end doesn't.

And, to the man I saw in the corridor that morning several years ago, if you are reading this I just want to say thank you. You made my day. And you make every day that I remember that one sentence that you said that taught me a very valuable lesson. I am eternally grateful.

# ~ LESSON 18 ~

## You *can* change the world

I've had a dream since I was little to do one "great" thing in my life. I didn't know what it was going to be, but I knew I wanted it to be something big. I wanted to change the world in a drastic way. As I got older and time went by, like my dream of writing, I set that thought aside.

I've been fortunate enough to run across some people that I've helped who have told me that I made a difference to them. I'm certainly not discounting that. I'm glad to be of service to people. That's where I find my life satisfaction…helping others.

But, after my move across country, I've found a lot of time on my hands to try to figure out exactly what I want to do with my life. Here enters my dream again. To do something big that benefits the world.

What do I do and how do I get the word out? It struck me like a bolt of lightning, and within forty-eight hours, my dream had come to life. I launched *Handcuffs of Hope*.

*Handcuffs of Hope* is my attempt to bring attention to the good things that happen in this world. You can't turn on the news or read the paper without having all of the rotten people front and center. It's time that the good people get front and center. And, I want to tell their stories.

I decided that my goal was to get everyone involved in making this world a better place. I want to change the world…one random act of kindness at a time.

It feels good to do things for other people. There's no greater satisfaction in my book than helping someone else. It may be something relatively minor like opening a door for someone on crutches. Or, it could be something bigger like helping someone that is struggling with a major life crisis, like losing someone close to them.

What makes me happy is to make other people happy. I suppose that's what led me into law enforcement. The desire to help other people.

I want to recognize those people that go out of their way to help others. I want to help them tell their stories and motivate and inspire others to do the same.

I was completely astonished when, less than twelve hours after creating my website and Facebook page, I had interest in the project from all over the world! I couldn't have had a brighter smile on my face!

New inquiries come in every day, people asking about *Handcuffs of Hope* and what they can do to help. "What can you do?" I answer. "Do a random act of kindness!"

So, here is my plea to you to join the movement and spread kindness. We all have struggles and we all have pain. It's time we all had joy too.

Just commit to a random act of kindness and, if you feel like sharing, send me your story at cdebusk13@gmail.com. I'll compile all of the submissions and publish them to help motivate others to do good things. Together, we can make a difference.

To those of you who already live the life of helper, my hats off to you. You are the heroes. You are the ones who make this world great. Thank you for all you do. I hope our paths cross at some point, more so than what they are doing right now. I'd love to hear your stories. Even if you don't want it published, drop me a line. I am a sucker for a good motivational story.

# ~ LESSON 19 ~

## It's all good

Here we are at the end of this book. I hope that my stories have helped you and inspired you to live the best life possible.

We all face times when we're down and struggle. That's part of being human. But, if we can keep those times to a minimum, why shouldn't we?

I have chosen "It's all good" as my last lesson in this book because this is something I say over and over again.

Do I believe it? I sure do. Life is good. It is very good.

So, when things have you down and you are just waiting for your struggles to pass, just smile, and say "It's all good."

You will see that it is.

All the best to you.

www.ingramcontent.com/pod-product-compliance
Lightning Source LLC
Chambersburg PA
CBHW070522030426
42337CB00016B/2070